The Complete Keto Diet for Beginners # 2019

Lose Weight, Balance Hormones, Boost Brain Health, and Reverse Disease

Dr. Jacob Banks

Table of contents

Introduction

The book you are holding in your hands helps guide you through the ketogenic diet and the various benefits related to it. The ketogenic diet helps to change your current eating habits into healthy ones. By adopting a keto lifestyle, you can eat natural, healthy, and delicious foods that are beneficial for your physical and mental health and also provides constant energy throughout your day. In this book, we explain the very basics related to your body and keto diet. The keto diet helps you to maintain your weight. People worried about excess weight often follow numerous diets for weight loss, taking weight-loss pills and drinking shakes and doing strenuous exercise, trying to achieve some nominal success. However, if dieting and exercising are difficult, these people often gain back all the weight they lost and sometimes even more.

The keto diet is one of the most effective ways to lose weight with less effort just by following keto diet rules. This book helps you to learn about the various benefits of the ketogenic diet, giving you the confidence and knowledge to lose weight and keep it off.

Chapter 1: Understanding the Keto Diet

The human body needs energy for performing day-to-day functions, and this energy comes in the form of carbohydrates, fats, and proteins. The ketogenic diet is a low-carb, high-fat, and moderate protein diet. Most of the energy our body depends on is glucose (carbohydrates). The keto diet forces your body to burn fat instead of carbohydrates, which are stored in the body in the form of glucose. Excess glucose is converted in the form of glycogens. When our body doesn't need glucose for energy, it is stored in muscles and the liver. This stored glucose is made up of connected glucose molecules called glycogens. When doing any physical activity or exercise, our body uses these stored glycogens as fuel.

Is Keto Right for You?

According to the latest research, the ketogenic diet can promote faster weight loss compared to other traditional low-fat diets. The keto diet is considered to be a low-carb diet due to its effective ability to maintain cholesterol, triglycerides, and blood sugar levels. The keto diet has long-term health benefits, including conditions like epilepsy, high blood pressure, heart disease, fatty liver disease, cancer, Alzheimer's disease, Parkinson's disease, acne, gout, autism and spectrum disorder. For example, research studies show that the keto diet is effective and safe for children who have epilepsy to follow.

The keto diet helps to meets your micronutrient needs. When you are on the diet, it is difficult to find a diet that provides you the necessary vitamins and minerals needed for your body to maintain its optimal health. The keto diet does this. The keto diet also helps to improve your overall health.

What Happens to Your Body When on the Keto Diet?

Normally, your body uses glucose as a primary source of energy. Glucose is derived from dietary carbs, and it comes from sugar and starchy foods. When your glucose level is high, your body stores excess glucose in the form of glycogens. These glycogens are stored in your liver and muscles. While you are following a ketogenic diet, you are reducing your carb consumption. This reduces the glycogen stored in your body along with the level of the hormone insulin. In this process, fatty acids released from stored fat in your body and liver convert into ketones.

Ketosis is a metabolic process. When your body does not have enough glucose for energy, your body breaks down fats for energy instead of glucose. The result of this is the buildup of acid in your body, called ketones. Ketones are a kind of acid that built up in your blood and is eliminated through urine. Ketones are used as an alternative energy source for your muscles. When you are doing any strenuous activity, ketone levels are increased.

How to Know Whether You Are in Ketosis

There are several methods to find out whether you are in ketosis which can be described as follows:

- Ketones in urine test: Normally, your body burns glucose as a primary energy source. When you are on the ketogenic diet, the glucose level in your body goes low due to this, your cells don't get enough glucose. In this condition, your body burns fat instead of glucose. This will produce ketones in your blood and urine. You can check urine ketone levels with the help of Ketostix. Ketostix is a brand name of ketone test strips that are an inexpensive and accurate way to check the ketone levels in urine. You can check your ketones levels using these sticks easily. You just need to collect urine in a clean container, and dip the stick into it, shake the stick to remove excess urine and wait for 15 seconds. After 15 seconds, the strip color should change, and you can follow the associated guide to check your ketosis level.

- Blood test: Blood test is one of the most accurate methods to measure ketone levels. This test is a little expensive, used by those afflicted with diabetes to measure blood ketone levels. Similar to a glucometer, you need ketone meter, ketone test strips, and lancet pen. After testing your blood, and the ketone meter displays between 0.5 and 3 mmol/L, then you are in ketosis.

- Ketosis breath: Ketosis breath, also known as keto breath, occurs when your body is in a state of ketosis, and fatty acids are being broken down in your kidneys and liver for energy. During this process, acetone is released, which can be smelled on your breath. Bad breath problems often occur within a few days after changing your diet to a keto-based diet. Having keto breath means your body is in a state of ketosis.

- **Increased thirst and dry mouth:** This condition happens during the keto diet due to a decrease in insulin level. Your body starts expelling excess sodium and water. Those following a keto diet are recommended to take 2 to 4 grams of sodium per day as part of your diet plan to balance your body's electrolyte levels. When your body enters into a state of ketosis, your body is using an excess number of glycogens. Due to this, your body increases the need for urination, which creates an increase in thirst. This is also a sign of your body being in ketosis.

Chapter 2: Ketogenic Diet Benefits

Many scientific studies prove that a ketogenic diet has various health benefits, such as the following:

- Burns stored body fats: Normally, your body uses glucose as a primary energy source. When your body enters into ketosis, your body burns fats for energy instead of glucose. In your body, extra glucose is stored in the form of glycogens. Excess glycogens are stored in the form of fats. Much of the research shows that the ketogenic diet is very effective for long-term weight-loss benefits.

- Helps to maintain blood sugar level: While following the keto diet, your body uses ketones as a primary energy source instead of glucose. This helps to maintain a stable blood sugar level throughout the day. Glucose needs insulin to transport into the blood cells. It also helps to increase insulin sensitivity. Ketones don't require insulin to transport, which means that the keto diet prevents insulin resistance. Due to this, your body's fuel levels stay steady all day.

- Improves your metabolic flexibility: Metabolic flexibility is one type of energy source required to function our body's cells. When you are eating normally, your body uses glucose as an energy source. However, when you are on the keto diet, your body burns fats as an energy source instead of glucose. These types of changes in your body's cells translate to metabolic flexibility. Ketones are the best alternative source of fuel for your brain. Metabolic flexibility helps your body to switch between carbs and fats easily.

- Improve your brain health: Ketones helps to improve your mental health and your brain functions. It also helps to improve your learning, focus, attention, and memory functions. Scientific research shows that ketosis is helpful in preventing or reducing the risk of Alzheimer's, neurodegeneration, epilepsy, and Parkinson's. When the glucose and insulin levels in your body are low, your liver produces ketones from fatty acids. Ketones provide 70 percent of your brain's energy needs.

- Improves heart functions: Ketones has an antioxidant property that helps protect the lining of your blood vessels. They also help boost your blood circulation, improve your heart function, and lower the risk of heart disease. One study proves that the keto diet improves heart efficiency by 30 percent and blood flow by 75 percent.

- Prevents various diseases: Ketones has antioxidant and anti-inflammatory properties that help to prevent various diseases like Alzheimer's, Parkinson's, cancer, obesity Huntington's, heart disease, epilepsy, and type-2 diabetes. One of the research studies proves that the keto diet improves 50 percent of epilepsy patients.

- Boost your physical exercise performance: Scientific research shows that compare to any other diet, the keto diet helps to reduce fat faster. The keto diet provides long-term health benefits. Adenosine triphosphate (ATP) is a high-energy molecule found in every cell. Compared to ATP, ketones produce more energy. The study also shows that intramuscular fat-burning process is 20 times faster in the keto diet. Ketones are beneficial for endurance athletes as during resistance training, you lose only fat, not muscle. It helps to maintain your muscle mass and boost your physical exercise performance. Various studies show ketones in the blood can improve your performance significantly.

- Anti-aging: The keto diet decrease insulin levels and allow your body to use ketones as a fuel. Lowering insulin levels and oxidative stress in the body may also help to increase your lifespan. During the research, study researchers found that during starvation, the human body produces one of the chemical compounds called beta-hydroxybutyrate plays an important role in the aging process. Previous research shows that calorie restriction can slow down the aging process and increase longevity as well.

- Increase the level of HDL: High-density lipoprotein (HDL), or good cholesterol, can increase while following the keto diet. An increase in the level of HDL relative to low-density lipoprotein (LDL), or bad cholesterol, helps to lower the risk of heart disease. The keto diet is basically a low-carb, high-fat diet. One of the best ways to increase your HDL level is eating foods high in fat. HDL levels are increased in the low-carb diet plan.

- Increase mitochondrial functions: Every cell of the body contains mitochondria, which is responsible for creating 90 percent of the energy needed by your body. Mitochondria works like cell energy factories. The keto diet helps to increase the energetic output of mitochondria. Mitochondria use fat for energy, so the status of your mitochondria in your body is an indicator of your overall your health.

Chapter 3: Foods to Eat

Below, you will find a ketogenic diet-friendly food list. Always use grass-fed meat and organic meat while you are on a keto diet. Unprocessed meats are low-carb meats, which means that they are keto-friendly. Do not take in a huge amount of meat because it is also high in protein. Keto is a high-fat diet, not high-protein diet. Always use a normal amount of protein.

- Beef: Ground beef, stew meat, steak, and roasts

- Pork: Pork chops, ground pork, pork loin, ham, and tenderloins

- Other meats: Goat, veal, turkey, and lamb
- Seafood & fish: Most fish and seafood are good in the keto diet, especially fatty fish. Wild-caught fish and shellfish are the best choices.
  - Fish: Salmon, catfish, flounder, cod, halibut, mahi-mahi, trout, tuna and mackerel
  - Shellfish: Lobster, crab, clams, oyster, mussels, squid and scallops
- Eggs: Pastured and organic eggs are the healthiest options in the keto diet. You can prepare eggs in a variety of ways like boiled, fried, poached, deviled, and scrambled.

- Vegetables & fruits: Leafy and green vegetables are the best option for the keto diet. Vegetables are a tasty way to eat fat while following the keto diet. Vegetables help to add flavors and colors to your keto meal. Vegetables are low in carbohydrates and high in nutrients. Always use nonstarchy vegetables.

- Vegetables: Spinach, radicchio, chives, kale, kohlrabi, cucumber, asparagus, and summer squash.

- Fruit: Avocado.

- Dairy products: Use high-fat dairy products like butter, cheese, yogurt, and heavy cream. Avoid low-fat dairy products because it contains added sugar.

- Oil & fats: Fat is necessary for the keto diet because most of the calories come from fat. Fats like butter, coconut fats, olive oil, avocado oil, and nut butters are the best options on the keto diet.

- Beverages & condiments: Tea, coffee, pickles, mustard, mayonnaise, bone broths, and fermented foods are allowed on the keto diet as are all herbs and spices, lime juice, lime zest, and whey protein.

Chapter 4: Foods to Avoid

- Added sugar: A sweetener causes a rise in your blood sugar levels along with insulin spikes. Cut off all fruit juices, soft drinks, vitamin water, and sports drinks that contain sugar. Also avoid candy, cakes, donuts, chocolate bars, and breakfast cereals along with hidden sugars, especially in condiments, dressings, sauces, drinks, and packaged foods. Maple syrup, honey, and agave also contain sugars. Avoid artificial sweeteners too.

- Starchy food: Starchy foods are high in carbohydrates. The list of foods to avoid are potatoes, pasta, rice, bread, potato chips, porridge, french fries, and similar items.

- Dairy products: Milk should be avoided because it is difficult to digest, due to the lack of good bacteria.

- Legumes: Legumes like lentils, peanuts, chickpeas, and beans should be avoided on the keto diet because of the high carbs. Legumes also contain phytates and lectins that are hard to digest.

- Tropical fruits: Avoid tropical fruits like pineapples, bananas, mangoes, tangerines, and grapes because they are high in sugar and carbs. Avoid fruit juices completely.

- Refined oils: Avoid refined oils and fats like sunflower oil, corn oil, canola oil, and soybean oil. Margarine is also on the list due to being high in trans fats.

- Processed food: Completely avoid processed food like almond milk products, sulfites like dried fruits, and anything containing monosodium glutamate (MSG) or wheat protein.

- Wheat gluten and soy products: You should be aware of bisphenol A (BPA)-lined cans because it has some negative effect on your health, such as impaired thyroid function and cancer.

Chapter 5: Common Mistakes for Beginners

Below are some of the common mistakes made by people when beginning the ketogenic diet.

- **Comparing yourself to others:** Stop comparing to other people because everyone is different. When comparing yourself to others when dieting, you are likely to stress yourself out about the diet and have trouble focusing on it. Stress has a major impact on your body. If you are stressed constantly, you may notice that your body weight doesn't decrease —even when on a diet —and can even increase. When you are on the keto diet, your body reacts differently than others do, so it is pointless to compare yourself to someone else. Focus on your diet plan. If your goal is losing weight, then don't panic. The weight will come off.

- **Not consuming enough fats:** The keto diet is a low-carb, high-fat diet, so you need to consume enough fats. You may have to consume a large number of fats to reach your goal. About 75 percent of the food you consume needs to come from fat. It may seem counter-intuitive but, if you want to lose fat from your body, you should consume fats to do so when on the keto diet. If you are following a low-carb diet without consuming enough fats, this likely means that you are getting calories from protein. This can prevent you from entering ketosis. Always consume good fats like eggs, butter, coconut oil, and others. You should never be afraid to consume enough fats on this diet.

- **Eating too much protein:** The keto diet is a high-fat, low-carb diet that requires a moderate amount of protein diet. Some people consume as much protein as fat on this diet, causing the weight-loss process to slow down. Consuming enough protein is very important when on this diet for ensuring that your muscles function properly. If you consume too much protein while on the keto diet, your body will convert the excess protein into glucose, and your body uses this glucose as a primary energy source instead of burning fat. This may prevent you from entering ketosis or even cause you to fall out of ketosis.

- **Obsessing about the scale:** Weight scales are an important piece of equipment when on any diet because it is a simple way to track your progress. The problem comes when you are checking your weight frequently, such as multiple times daily, and you note no progress. It may lead to an increase in stress and cause you to lose motivation. The numbers on the scale are not the most indicative piece of information you have to tell whether the diet is working. Don't panic about the numbers on the scale because the scale doesn't show how your body is changing and how healthy your body is.

- Consuming the wrong fats: Always be careful about your fat intake. The keto diet requires lots of fats to be consumed, but they must be the right kind of fats. If you consume highly processed foods that have a high fat content, this will cause you certain health problems, such as a spike in your LDL cholesterol level or an increase the risk of heart disease or cancer. Therefore, stay away from processed fats. While you are on a keto diet, you should consume saturated fats, polyunsaturated fats, and monounsaturated fats.

- Not enough water: When you are on the keto diet, your body loses a lot of fluids and electrolytes, so it is important to stay your body hydrated through drinking enough water. If you stay hydrated, your body will be working smooth and well-oiled machine. When you are switching yourself to following the keto diet lifestyle, your body needs more water. It is recommended that you need to consume a gallon of water per day when following this diet.

- Lack of electrolytes: Normally, when you try to lose your weight, you often reduce your salt intake because it causes inflammation in your body. While on the keto diet, your body needs more salt in your food because your kidneys are flushing the sodium from your body at a high rate. In addition to sodium, you need to increase your consumption of magnesium and potassium, which are also important minerals for the body. A lack of sodium, magnesium, and potassium increases the chances you will get the keto flu. You can get plenty of potassium by consuming avocados and leafy vegetables while walnuts, pistachios, and almonds are a good source of magnesium.

Chapter 6: Can I Work Out on the Keto Diet?

One of the main benefits of the keto diet is that you can lose your body fat without working out at all. You never need to change your lifestyle to lose fats. You just need to change your eating habits.

However, the answer to this question is that you can work out on the keto diet without experiencing a loss of physical performance. Many people think that a high amount of carbs provide your body the energy that it needs to push throughout strenuous exercise. While this is correct in theory, you consume fewer carbs when following the keto diet, which seems like it could be an issue. However, the good news is that even if you work out while following the keto diet, your body doesn't need extra carbs. Your body consumes the energy you need by burning fats, meaning you feel any more fatigued from a workout than when eating normally.

There are four types of exercise you can do while in ketosis:

- Aerobic exercises: These exercises are lower in intensity, allowing you to have a steady state of fat burning. Also known as cardio exercise, aerobic exercises typically only occur in bursts of a few minutes, making them ideal for keto dieters.

- Anaerobic exercises: Weightlifting and sprinting are considered anaerobic exercise. These exercises are also characterized by short bursts of energy. The few carbs you to take in while on this diet are usually the main fuel in these exercises.

- Flexibility exercises: These exercises are helpful for supporting joints and stretching out your muscles. These exercises help prevent injuries caused by the shortening of the muscles over time. Yoga is a good example of this type of exercise.

- Stability exercises: These are balancing and core training exercises that can help to improve your body's alignment, provide added control of movement, and strengthen your muscles.

Chapter 7: FAQs

Where can I find low-carb recipes?

In addition to the many low-carb recipes that we have included in this book, you can find low-carb recipes on the internet on various health-related websites. You can also conduct an internet browser search that can help you locate additional low-carb recipes.

How long does it take to get into ketosis?

It takes time for your body to adjust to this new way of eating and enter a state of ketosis. Normally, it takes between two and seven days to enter into ketosis. This depends on your body type, eating habits, and activity levels. Exercising on an empty stomach is one of the fastest ways to get into ketosis.

How should I track my carb intake?

You can track your carb intake through MyFitnessPal and similar mobile apps. Using this app, you can track your total carb and fiber intake. You cannot track net carbs through the app, however. To calculating net carbs, subtract your total fiber intake from total carb intake, which will give you the net carb value.

Can I eat too much fat?

Yes, you can eat too much fat while on the keto diet. Eating too much fat will push you into a calorie deficit, creating a calorie surplus. You can use a keto calculator to calculate macros and see how much fats, carbs, and proteins you should consume in a day based on your body type.

How will I know I am in ketosis?

The most common and inexpensive way to know you are in ketosis is by using Ketostix. These can confirm that you are in ketosis. Ketostix results are not 100 percent accurate, however, because they only measure the amount of acetones in your urine. The ketones used by your body for energy are called as beta-hydroxybutyrate, which is not measured by using Ketostix. A more accurate and reliable way to measure your ketone levels is through a blood ketone meter. A ketone meter shows the exact number of ketones in your blood, but these can be a bit pricey.

Is the keto diet effective for weight loss?

The keto diet allows you to maintain a caloric deficit without hunger, which gives you better access to fat stores, which is one of the reasons the keto diet is one of the most effective diets for weight loss.

Who should not attempt a keto diet?

This diet guide does not offer medical advice, and you should discuss your nutritional strategies with your doctor before beginning any diet, including the keto diet. However, ketosis is not recommended for anyone with the following conditions:

- Beta oxidation defects
- CPT I/II deficiency
- Kidney failure
- Pregnancy
- Carnitine deficiency
- Type 1 diabetes
- Gallbladders disease
- Impaired fat digestion
- Impaired liver function
- Abdominal tumors
- Impaired gastrointestinal motility
- Gastric bypass surgery
- Pancreatitis

Chapter 8: Meal Plans
Week One Meal Plan

Day 1

- **Breakfast**: Veggies & Sausage Muffins
- **Lunch**: Easy Beef Bowl
- **Dinner**: Crispy Chicken Tenders

Day 2

- **Breakfast**: Delicious Breakfast Casserole
- **Lunch**: Shredded Chicken
- **Dinner**: Thai Beef Curry

Day 3

- **Breakfast**: Super Easy Breakfast Casserole
- **Lunch**: Flavorful Meatballs
- **Dinner**: Chicken Drumsticks

Day 4

- **Breakfast**: Thick & Fluffy Pancakes
- **Lunch**: Basil Tomato Shrimp
- **Dinner**: Beef Chili

Day 5

- **Breakfast**: Breakfast Meatloaf
- **Lunch**: Parmesan Pork Chops
- **Dinner**: Cilantro Lime Salmon

Day 6

- **Breakfast**: Tomato Basil Frittata
- **Lunch**: Mediterranean Fish Fillets

- **Dinner**: Easy Onion Pork Chops

Day 7

- **Breakfast**: Coconut Waffles
- **Lunch**: Beef Stew
- **Dinner**: Lemon Parmesan Shrimp

Week Two Meal Plan

Day 1

- **Breakfast:** Spinach Artichoke Casserole
- **Lunch:** Broccoli Soup
- **Dinner:** Grilled Lamb Kababs

Day 2

- **Breakfast:** Super Easy Breakfast Casserole
- **Lunch:** Tomato Carrot Soup
- **Dinner:** Basil Pesto Salmon

Day 3

- **Breakfast:** Breakfast Meatloaf
- **Lunch:** Chicken Ranch Salad
- **Dinner:** Delicious Chicken Curry

Day 4

- **Breakfast:** Coconut Waffles
- **Lunch:** Air-fried Meatballs
- **Dinner:** Dijon Lamb Chops

Day 5

- **Breakfast:** Tomato Basil Frittata
- **Lunch:** Garlic Mushroom Soup
- **Dinner:** Mushroom Garlic Chicken

Day 6

- **Breakfast:** Thick & Fluffy Pancakes
- **Lunch:** Healthy Cauliflower Spinach Soup
- **Dinner:** Lemon Garlic Lamb Chops

Day 7

- **Breakfast**: Delicious Breakfast Casserole
- **Lunch**: Creamy Cauliflower Soup
- **Dinner**: Italian Pot Roast

Week Three Meal Plan

Day 1

- **Breakfast**: Coconut Waffles
- **Lunch**: Chicken Ranch Salad
- **Dinner**: Italian Pot Roast

Day 2

- **Breakfast**: Tomato Basil Frittata
- **Lunch**: Lemon Garlic Shrimp
- **Dinner**: Delicious Chicken Curry

Day 3

- **Breakfast**: Breakfast Meatloaf
- **Lunch**: Mushroom Garlic Chicken
- **Dinner**: Basil Pesto Salmon

Day 4

- **Breakfast**: Thick & Fluffy Pancakes
- **Lunch**: Grilled Lamb Kababs
- **Dinner**: Chicken Drumsticks

Day 5

- **Breakfast**: Super Easy Breakfast Casserole
- **Lunch**: Easy Beef Bowl
- **Dinner**: Tomato Caper Chicken

Day 6

- **Breakfast**: Delicious Breakfast Casserole
- **Lunch**: Dijon Lamb Chops
- **Dinner**: Beef Stew

Day 7

- **Breakfast**: Veggies & Sausage Muffins
- **Lunch**: Lemon Garlic Lamb Chops
- **Dinner**: Beef Chili

Chapter 9: Breakfast

Veggies & Sausage Muffins

Preparation Time: 10 minutes

Cooking Time: 20 minutes

Serve: 12

Ingredients:

- 9 eggs
- ¼ cup coconut milk
- ½ teaspoon dried oregano
- 1½ cups spinach
- ½ cup bell peppers, chopped
- ½ onion, sliced
- 1 tablespoon olive oil
- 8 ounces breakfast sausage, crumbled
- Ground black pepper, to taste
- Salt, to taste

Directions:

1. Preheat the oven to 180C/350F.
2. Spray muffin tray with cooking spray and set aside.
3. Add crumbled sausage to the pan and cook over medium-high heat. Once sausage is cooked halfway, then add oil, oregano, bell peppers, and onions to the pan and sauté until onions are softened.
4. Add spinach and stir well. Cover pan with lid and cook for 30 seconds.
5. Remove the lid and stir everything well. Remove pan from heat.
6. In a large bowl, whisk eggs with milk, black pepper, and salt.
7. Add sausage and veggie mixture to the egg mixture and mix well.

8. Pour egg mixture to the prepared muffin tray and bake in preheated oven for 20 minutes.

9. Serve and enjoy.

Nutritional Value (Amount per Serving):

- Calories 137
- Fat 11 g
- Carbohydrates 1.5 g
- Sugar 0.9 g
- Protein 8.2 g
- Cholesterol 139 mg

Delicious Breakfast Casserole

Preparation Time: 10 minutes

Cooking Time: 50 minutes

Serve: 8

Ingredients:

- 12 eggs
- ½ cup cheddar cheese, shredded
- 3 cups fresh spinach, chopped
- ½ onion, diced
- 2 cups bell peppers, diced
- ½ tablespoon garlic, minced
- 1 pound ground breakfast sausage
- Ground black pepper, to taste
- Salt, to taste

Directions:

1. Preheat the oven to 180C/350F.
2. Spray baking dish with cooking spray and set aside.
3. Cook ground sausage in a pan over medium heat until fully cooked.
4. Add onions, black peppers, and garlic to the sausage pan and sauté for 2 minutes. Transfer on a prepared baking dish.
5. Top with chopped spinach.
6. Whisk eggs in a bowl with black pepper and salt and pour egg mixture over spinach in baking dish.
7. Sprinkle with shredded cheddar cheese and bake in preheated oven for 45 minutes.
8. Serve and enjoy.

Nutritional Value (Amount per Serving):

- Calories 236
- Fat 15 g
- Carbohydrates 4.1 g
- Sugar 2.4 g
- Protein 20.8 g
- Cholesterol 297 mg

Super Easy Breakfast Casserole

Preparation Time: 10 minutes

Cooking Time: 55 minutes

Serve: 8

Ingredients:

- 6 eggs
- ¼ teaspoon Italian seasoning
- 1 cup cheddar cheese, shredded
- 1 cup mozzarella cheese, shredded
- 1 pound ground pork sausage
- Ground black pepper, to taste
- Salt, to taste

Directions:

1. Preheat the oven to 180C/350F.
2. Spray 9-inch pie pan with cooking spray and set aside.
3. Cook ground sausage in a pan over medium-high heat until brown. Drain sausage well and let it cool.
4. In a bowl, whisk together eggs, shredded cheese, and Italian seasoning.
5. Mix sausage and egg mixture until well combined.
6. Pour mixture into the prepared pie pan and bake in preheated oven for 55 minutes.
7. Serve and enjoy.

Nutritional Value (Amount per Serving):

- Calories 268
- Fat 20.7 g
- Carbohydrates 2 g
- Sugar 0.3 g
- Protein 17.4 g

Thick & Fluffy Pancakes

Preparation Time: 10 minutes

Cooking Time: 10 minutes

Serve: 5

Ingredients:

- 4 eggs
- 2 tablespoons Swerve
- 1 teaspoon baking powder
- ½ teaspoon vanilla extract
- ¼ cup water
- 1 tablespoon coconut oil
- ½ cup butter, melted
- 2 cups almond flour
- Pinch of salt

Directions:

1. Add all ingredients into the blender and blend until well combined.
2. Spray pan with cooking spray and heat over medium heat.
3. Pour 1/3 cup pancake batter on hot pan and make a round pancake.
4. Cook pancake until edges are firm. Flip to other side and cook for a minute.
5. Make remaining pancake using the same steps.

Nutritional Value (Amount per Serving):

- Calories 497
- Fat 47 g
- Carbohydrates 11.2 g
- Sugar 1.9 g
- Protein 14.2 g
- Cholesterol 180mg

Breakfast Meatloaf

Preparation Time: 10 minutes

Cooking Time: 35 minutes

Serve: 4

Ingredients:

- 6 eggs
- 2 tablespoons green onions, chopped
- 1 cup cheddar cheese, shredded
- 4 ounces cream cheese
- ¼ cup onion, chopped
- 1 pound ground sausage

Directions:
1. Preheat the oven to 180C/350F.
2. Spray a loaf pan with cooking spray and set aside.
3. In a large mixing bowl, beat the eggs.
4. Add onion, sausage, and half of the cream cheese, and mix well.
5. Pour egg mixture into the loaf pan and bake in preheated oven for 30 minutes.
6. Remove loaf pan from oven and let it cool for 5 minutes.
7. Spread remaining cream cheese on top of meatloaf then top with shredded cheese and green onion.
8. Bake for 5 minutes more.
9. Remove from oven and let it cool for 5 minutes.
10. Slice and serve.

Nutritional Value (Amount per Serving):

- Calories 695
- Fat 58 g
- Carbohydrates 2.5 g
- Sugar 1.1 g
- Protein 39.6 g

Tomato Basil Frittata

Preparation Time: 10 minutes

Cooking Time: 10 minutes

Serve: 2

Ingredients:

- 6 eggs
- 1 tablespoon butter
- 3 ounces cherry tomatoes, halved
- 2/3 cup feta cheese, crumbled
- 1 tablespoon fresh basil, chopped
- 1 onion, chopped
- Ground black pepper, to taste
- Salt, to taste

Directions:

1. Preheat the broiler to 200C/400F.
2. Melt butter in a pan over medium-high heat.
3. Add onion and sauté until onion is lightly browned.
4. In a bowl, whisk together eggs, basil, black pepper, and salt.
5. Pour egg mixture into a pan.
6. Top with cherry tomatoes and crumbled cheese.
7. Place pan in preheated broiler and cook for 5 to 7 minutes.

Nutritional Value (Amount per Serving):

- Calories 402
- Fat 29.7 g
- Carbohydrates 9.9 g
- Sugar 6.5 g
- Protein 24.8 g
- Cholesterol 551 mg

Coconut Waffles

Preparation Time: 10 minutes

Cooking Time: 20 minutes

Serve: 5

Ingredients:

- 5 eggs, separated
- 3 tablespoons coconut milk
- 1 teaspoon vanilla extract
- ¼ cup coconut flour
- 4 ounces butter, melted
- 1 teaspoon baking powder
- 3 tablespoons Swerve

Directions:

1. In a large bowl, beat egg whites until stiff peaks form.
2. In another bowl, add egg yolks, baking powder, Swerve, and coconut flour. Mix well.
3. Slowly add melted butter and stir well.
4. Add vanilla extract and coconut milk. Stir well.
5. Add egg whites and fold gently.
6. Pour batter into preheated waffle iron and cook the waffles until lightly golden.

Nutritional Value (Amount per Serving):

- Calories 256
- Fat 25 g
- Carbohydrates 3 g
- Sugar 0.8 g
- Protein 6 g
- Cholesterol 212 mg

Spinach Artichoke Casserole

Preparation Time: 10 minutes

Cooking Time: 30 minutes

Serve: 12

Ingredients:

- 16 eggs
- 14-ounce can artichoke hearts, drained and cut into pieces
- 10 ounces frozen spinach, thawed and drained
- 2 garlic cloves, minced
- ¼ cup onion, shaved
- ½ cup ricotta cheese
- ½ cup Parmesan cheese, grated
- ½ teaspoon red pepper, crushed
- ½ teaspoon thyme, diced
- 1 cup cheddar cheese, shredded
- ¼ cup coconut milk
- 1 teaspoon salt

Directions:

1. Preheat the oven to 180C/350F.
2. Spray baking dish with cooking spray and set aside.
3. In a large bowl, whisk together eggs and coconut milk.
4. Add spinach and artichoke into the egg mixture.
5. Add all remaining ingredients except ricotta cheese and stir well to combine.
6. Pour egg mixture into the prepared baking dish.
7. Spread ricotta cheese on top of egg mixture.
8. Bake in preheated oven for 30 minutes.
9. Serve and enjoy.

Nutritional Value (Amount per Serving):

- Calories 216
- Fat 14.1 g
- Carbohydrates 4.7 g
- Sugar 1.4 g
- Protein 16.4 g
- Cholesterol 241 mg

Chapter 10: Appetizers & Snacks
Tasty Butter Crackers

Preparation Time: 10 minutes

Cooking Time: 15 minutes

Serve: 25

Ingredients:

- 2 egg whites
- 2¼ cups almond flour
- ½ cup butter, softened
- Salt, to taste

Directions:

1. Preheat the oven to 180C/350F.
2. In a mixing bowl, combine almond flour and butter using a hand mixer.
3. Add egg whites and salt and mix on low speed until smooth dough is formed.
4. Roll dough between the two parchment paper pieces. Make sure dough thickness is 1/8 inch.
5. Cut dough into square pieces using a sharp knife.
6. Bake crackers in preheated oven for 10 to 15 minutes.
7. Remove from oven and allow to cool completely.
8. Serve and enjoy.

Nutritional Value (Amount per Serving):

- Calories 92
- Fat 8.7 g
- Carbohydrates 2.2 g
- Sugar 0.4 g
- Protein 2.5 g
- Cholesterol 10 mg

Herb Crackers

Preparation Time: 10 minutes

Cooking Time: 15 minutes

Serve: 40

Ingredients:

- 1 egg
- ¼ cup butter
- 2 teaspoons garlic powder
- 1 tablespoon Italian herbs
- ¼ cup coconut flour
- ¼ cup almond flour
- 2 tablespoons sour cream
- 1¾ cup mozzarella cheese, shredded
- 1 teaspoon salt

Directions:

1. Preheat the oven to 200C/400F.
2. Melt mozzarella cheese in a pan over medium heat.
3. Remove from heat. Add sour cream and stir until well combined.
4. In a large bowl, mix 1 teaspoon garlic powder, Italian herb, egg, coconut flour, almond flour, and cheese mixture until well combined.
5. Cover dough with plastic wrap and place in refrigerator for 10 minutes.
6. Melt butter in a pan over medium heat.
7. Add garlic powder and ½ teaspoon of salt in melted butter and simmer for 5 minutes.
8. Roll dough between two parchment paper pieces and cut into shapes using a sharp knife.
9. Brush crackers top using melted butter mixture and bake in preheated oven for 12 to 15 minutes.

10. Remove crackers from oven and allow to cool completely.
11. Serve and enjoy.

Nutritional Value (Amount per Serving):

- Calories 22
- Fat 2 g
- Carbohydrates 0.4 g
- Sugar 0.1 g
- Protein 0.7 g
- Cholesterol 8 mg

Healthy Broccoli Balls

Preparation Time: 10 minutes

Cooking Time: 25 minutes

Serve: 20

Ingredients:

- 2 eggs
- 1 teaspoon Italian seasoning
- 1 garlic clove, minced
- 1 cup cheddar cheese, shredded
- ¼ cup onion, minced
- ½ cup almond flour
- 2 cups broccoli florets
- Ground black pepper, to taste
- Salt, to taste

Directions:

1. Preheat the oven to 200C/400F.
2. Line baking tray with parchment paper and set aside.
3. Steam broccoli florets in boiling water until tender. Drain well and finely chop with a knife.
4. In a large bowl, mix broccoli, eggs, cheese, almond flour, onion, garlic, and spices until well combined.
5. Take a tablespoon of mixture and form into a ball and place on lined baking tray. Make remaining broccoli balls and arrange on baking tray.
6. Bake in preheated oven for 25 to 30 minutes.
7. Serve and enjoy.

Nutritional Value (Amount per Serving):

- Calories 50

- Fat 3.8 g
- Carbohydrates 1.5 g
- Sugar 0.4 g
- Protein 2.8 g
- Cholesterol 22 mg

Crunchy Tortilla Chips

Preparation Time: 10 minutes

Cooking Time: 8 minutes

Serve: 8

Ingredients:

- ¾ cup almond flour
- ¼ teaspoon onion powder
- ¼ teaspoon garlic powder
- 2 teaspoons psyllium husk powder
- 2 cups mozzarella cheese, shredded
- Pinch of salt

Directions:

1. Preheat the oven to 180C/350F.
2. Melt shredded mozzarella cheese in the microwave.
3. Once cheese is melted, add almond flour, spices, salt, and psyllium husk and knead dough until smooth.
4. Roll dough thinly and cut into triangle shapes using a sharp knife.
5. Arrange tortilla chips on a baking tray and bake in preheated oven for 8 minutes.
6. Serve and enjoy.

Nutritional Value (Amount per Serving):

- Calories 83
- Fat 6.5 g
- Carbohydrates 3.3 g
- Sugar 0.4 g
- Protein 4.3 g
- Cholesterol 4 mg

Easy Cheese Balls

Preparation Time: 10 minutes

Cooking Time: 10 minutes

Serve: 10

Ingredients:

- 1¾ cups cooked bacon, crumbled
- 8 ounces cream cheese, softened
- 8 ounces cheddar cheese, shredded

Directions:

1. Microwave bacon for 30 seconds and place in a dish.
2. Mix cheddar cheese and cream cheese.
3. Scoop cheese mixture ball using small cookie scoop and roll in bacon crumbles.
4. Arrange cheese balls on a plate and place in refrigerator.
5. Serve and enjoy.

Nutritional Value (Amount per Serving):

- Calories 269
- Fat 21 g
- Carbohydrates 0.9 g
- Sugar 0.2 g
- Protein 15.8 g
- Cholesterol 63 mg

Almond & Seed Crackers

Preparation Time: 10 minutes

Cooking Time: 9 hours, 10 minutes

Serve: 20

Ingredients:

- 3 tablespoons almonds
- 2 tablespoons shelled hemp seeds
- 3 tablespoons sunflower seeds
- 2 tablespoons flaxseeds
- ½ onion, minced
- 1 teaspoon salt

Directions:

1. Mix almonds and seeds and soak well.
2. Drain almonds and seeds well. Add all ingredients into the blender and blend until sticky.
3. Spread blended mixture onto a baking sheet evenly.
4. Dehydrate for 2 hours at 50C/125F, then 6 hours at 40C/105F.
5. Flip the sheet and finish with 1 hour at 40C/105F.
6. Slice and serve.

Nutritional Value (Amount per Serving):

- Calories 18
- Fat 1.4 g
- Carbohydrates 0.9 g
- Sugar 0.3 g
- Protein 0.8 g
- Cholesterol 0 mg

Healthy Flaxseed Chips

Preparation Time: 10 minutes

Cooking Time: 15 minutes

Serve: 8

Ingredients:

- 1 cup flaxseed meal
- ¾ teaspoon chili powder
- 1½ teaspoons onion powder
- 1½ teaspoons garlic powder
- ½ cup water
- ½ teaspoon cayenne
- ½ teaspoon paprika
- ½ cup water

Directions:

1. In a large bowl, mix ground flax meal and seasoning.
2. Add water and stir well to combine. Cover and set aside for 10 minutes.
3. Preheat the oven to 200C/400F.
4. Roll dough between two parchment papers pieces until rich desired thickness.
5. Place rolled dough with parchment paper onto a baking tray and cut into cracker sized pieces.
6. Bake in preheated oven for 15 minutes.
7. Allow to cool completely, then serve.

Nutritional Value (Amount per Serving):
- Calories 80
- Fat 4.5 g
- Carbohydrates 5.3 g
- Sugar 0.6 g
- Protein 2.9 g

Simple Tomatillo Salsa

Preparation Time: 5 minutes

Cooking Time: 5 minutes

Serve: 8

Ingredients:

- 4 tomatillos, chopped
- 1 green onion, minced
- ½ jalapeno pepper, chopped
- ¼ onion, chopped
- ½ teaspoon garlic powder
- ¼ cup fresh cilantro, chopped
- Salt, to taste

Directions:

1. In a bowl, mix tomatillos, garlic powder, cilantro, scallion, jalapeno pepper, and onion.
2. Season with salt and mix well.
3. Serve and enjoy.

Nutritional Value (Amount per Serving):

- Calories 8
- Fat 0.1 g
- Carbohydrates 1.5 g
- Sugar 0.3 g
- Protein 0.3 g
- Cholesterol 0 mg

Kale Spread

Preparation Time: 10 minutes

Cooking Time: 10 minutes

Serve: 10

Ingredients:

- 5 cups kale, chopped
- ½ cup olive oil
- 1 tablespoon coconut oil
- 6 green onions
- 2 tablespoons apple cider vinegar
- ½ cup hemp hearts
- 1¼ teaspoon sea salt

Directions:

1. Heat oil in a pan over low heat.
2. Add kale to the hot oil and sauté for 5 to 7 minutes.
3. Transfer kale into a food processor along with remaining ingredients and process until smooth.
4. Serve and enjoy.

Nutritional Value (Amount per Serving):

- Calories 168
- Fat 14.9 g
- Carbohydrates 5.9 g
- Sugar 0.3 g
- Protein 4.1 g
- Cholesterol 0 mg

Tasty Salsa

Preparation Time: 10 minutes

Cooking Time: 5 minutes

Serve: 4

Ingredients:

- 5 tomatoes, diced
- 1 jalapeno pepper, diced
- ¼ cup onion, chopped
- 3 tablespoons fresh cilantro, chopped
- Ground black pepper, to taste
- Salt, to taste

Directions:

1. Add tomatoes, cilantro, jalapeno, and onion into the bowl and mix well.
2. Season with black pepper and salt.
3. Serve and enjoy.

Nutritional Value (Amount per Serving):

- Calories 26
- Fat 0.3 g
- Carbohydrates 5.7 g
- Sugar 3.6 g
- Protein 1.2 g
- Cholesterol 0 mg

Chapter 11: Beef, Pork & Lamb

Easy Beef Bowl

Preparation Time: 10 minutes

Cooking Time: 15 minutes

Serve: 4

Ingredients:

- 1 pound ground beef
- 4 garlic cloves, minced
- 2 tablespoons coconut aminos
- ¼ cup coconut oil
- ¼ cup green onions, chopped
- 3 tablespoons fresh ginger, grated
- 1 onion, chopped

Directions:

1. Heat oil in a large pan over high heat.
2. Add onion to the pan and sauté until softened, about 5 minutes.
3. Add garlic and sauté for a minute.
4. Add meat and cook until meat is no pinker, about 8 minutes.
5. Add ginger and coconut aminos and simmer for 2 to 3 minutes.
6. Garnish with green onion and serve.

Nutritional Value (Amount per Serving):

- Calories 342
- Fat 20.7 g
- Carbohydrates 3 g
- Sugar 0.2 g
- Protein 34.7 g
- Cholesterol 101 mg

Thai Beef Curry

Preparation Time: 10 minutes

Cooking Time: 2 hours

Serve: 6

Ingredients:

- 2½ pounds chuck steak, cubed
- ½ lime zest
- ½ lime juice
- 14 ounces coconut cream
- 1 teaspoon ground turmeric
- ¼ cup beef broth
- 2 tablespoons curry paste
- ½ teaspoon salt

Directions:

1. Preheat the oven to 200C/400F.
2. In a large bowl, whisk together broth, lime juice, lime zest, turmeric, curry paste, and salt until well combined.
3. Add coconut cream and meat and stir until meat is well coated.
4. Pour mixture into a baking dish and cover with lid.
5. Bake in preheated oven for 2 hours.
6. Stir well and serve.

Nutritional Value (Amount per Serving):

- Calories 663
- Fat 43.6 g
- Carbohydrates 5.4 g
- Sugar 2.3 g
- Protein 60.7 g

Flavorful Meatballs

Preparation Time: 10 minutes

Cooking Time: 15 minutes

Serve: 8

Ingredients:

- ½ pound ground lamb meat
- ½ teaspoon dried oregano
- ½ teaspoon cumin
- 1 teaspoon coriander
- 2 tablespoons mint, minced
- 2 tablespoons parsley, minced
- 1 lemon juice
- 1 lemon zest, grated
- 3 garlic cloves, minced
- ¼ cup onion, grated
- 1 egg
- 3 tablespoons almond flour
- 1 pound ground beef
- ¼ teaspoon ground black pepper
- ¾ teaspoon sea salt

Directions:

1. Preheat the oven to 230C/450F.
2. Spray a baking tray with cooking spray and set aside.
3. Add all ingredients into the large mixing bowl and mix until well combined.
4. Make small balls from mixture and place on prepared baking tray and bake in preheated oven for 15 to 17 minutes.
5. Serve and enjoy.

Nutritional Value (Amount per Serving):

- Calories 201
- Fat 9.3 g
- Carbohydrates 1.7 g
- Sugar 0.3 g
- Protein 26.6 g
- Cholesterol 97 mg

Beef Chili

Preparation Time: 10 minutes

Cooking Time: 30 minutes

Serve: 6

Ingredients:

- 2 pounds ground beef
- 1 cup chicken broth
- 1½ teaspoons paprika
- 1 tablespoon olive oil
- ½ teaspoon oregano
- 1 tablespoon cumin
- 1½ tablespoons chili powder
- 3 ounces tomato paste
- 14.5-ounce can tomato, diced
- 5 bacon slices, cooked and crumbled
- 3 garlic cloves, minced
- 1 jalapeno pepper, chopped
- ½ cup celery, chopped
- 1 onion, chopped
- 1 bell pepper, chopped
- Ground black pepper, to taste
- Salt, to taste

Directions:

1. Heat oil in a saucepan over medium-high heat.
2. Add onion, bell pepper, and celery to the pan and cook until tender.
3. Add ground meat and vegetables and cook until browned. Drain well.
4. Add garlic and jalapeno and cook for a minute.
5. Add chili powder, paprika, oregano, and cumin and stir for 30 seconds.

6. Add crumbled bacon and stir well.
7. Turn heat to low and add tomatoes, tomato paste, black pepper, and salt.
8. Add broth and stir well and simmer for 20 minutes.
9. Serve and enjoy.

Nutritional Value (Amount per Serving):

- Calories 429
- Fat 17.1 g
- Carbohydrates 12.5 g
- Sugar 6.4 g
- Protein 54.9 g
- Cholesterol 153 mg

Parmesan Pork Chops

Preparation Time: 10 minutes

Cooking Time: 17 minutes

Serve: 4

Ingredients:

- 1 pound pork chops, boneless
- ¼ cup butter
- ½ teaspoon garlic, minced
- ¼ tablespoon garlic powder
- ½ teaspoon rosemary
- ¼ cup Parmesan cheese
- Ground black pepper, to taste
- Salt, to taste

Directions:

1. Melt 2 tablespoons of butter in microwave-safe bowl.
2. Add garlic to the melted butter. Mix well and set aside.
3. In another bowl, mix Parmesan cheese, garlic powder, and rosemary.
4. Brush pork chops with melted butter from both the sides.
5. Coat pork chops with Parmesan cheese.
6. Melt remaining butter in a pan over medium heat.
7. Place pork chops in the pan and cook over medium-high heat for 5 to 8 minutes per side.

Nutritional Value (Amount per Serving):

- Calories 488
- Fat 41.1 g
- Carbohydrates 0.8 g
- Protein 27.6 g
- Cholesterol 132 mg

Easy Onion Pork Chops

Preparation Time: 10 minutes

Cooking Time: 45 minutes

Serve: 8

Ingredients:

- 2½ pounds pork chops
- 1 onion, sliced
- 2 teaspoons soy sauce
- 1¼ cup apple cider vinegar
- ½ cup olive oil

Directions:

1. Heat oil in a pan over medium heat.
2. Add pork chops to the pan and cook until brown.
3. Once pork chops are browned then add remaining ingredients and stir well.
4. Cover pan with lid and cook for 45 minutes.
5. Serve and enjoy.

Nutritional Value (Amount per Serving):

- Calories 576
- Fat 47.8 g
- Carbohydrates 1.7 g
- Sugar 0.8 g
- Protein 32.1 g
- Cholesterol 122 mg

Beef Stew

Preparation Time: 10 minutes

Cooking Time: 30 minutes

Serve: 3

Ingredients:

For the stew:

- 1 pound ground beef
- 2 tablespoons olive oil
- 1 teaspoon sweet paprika
- 1 teaspoon cumin
- ¼ cup onion, diced
- ½ teaspoon ground black pepper
- ½ teaspoon sea salt
- ½ cup parsley, chopped

For the sauce:

- 1 tablespoon olive oil
- 1 garlic clove, minced
- 3 tomatoes, chopped
- 1 tablespoon tomato paste

Directions:

1. In a bowl, mix ground beef, parsley, black pepper, sweet paprika, cumin, onion, and sea salt.
2. Heat olive oil in a pan over medium heat.
3. Pour bowl mixture in the pan and cook for 2 minutes on each side.
4. Remove pan from heat and set aside.
5. Add garlic and tomatoes into the blender and blend until smooth.

6. Return pan on heat. Pour tomato mixture and stir well.
7. Mix olive oil with tomato paste and add it to the pan mixture.
8. Cover pan with lid and cook for 25 minutes over medium heat.
9. Garnish with parsley and serve.

Nutritional Value (Amount per Serving):

- Calories 442
- Fat 24.1 g
- Carbohydrates 8.6 g
- Sugar 4.5 g
- Protein 47.9 g
- Cholesterol 135 mg

Grilled Lamb Kababs

Preparation Time: 10 minutes

Cooking Time: 15 minutes

Serve: 4

Ingredients:

- 1 pound ground lamb
- ¼ cup fresh parsley, chopped
- 2 garlic cloves, minced
- 1 medium onion, minced
- ⅛ teaspoon ground cloves
- ¼ teaspoon allspice
- ⅛ teaspoon cinnamon
- ¼ teaspoon ground black pepper
- ½ teaspoon salt

Directions:

1. Preheat the grill over medium-high heat.
2. In a bowl, add all ingredients and mix until well combined.
3. Divide mixture into four portions and shape each portion into sausage shape and thread onto a soaked wooden skewer.
4. Grill over hot grill for 10 minutes. Turn every 2 to 3 minutes.

Nutritional Value (Amount per Serving):

- Calories 226
- Fat 8.4 g
- Carbohydrates 3.4 g
- Sugar 1.2 g
- Protein 32.3 g
- Cholesterol 102 mg

Italian Pot Roast

Preparation Time: 10 minutes

Cooking Time: 45 minutes

Serve: 8

Ingredients:

- 3½ pounds beef chuck roast, cut into cubes
- 1 onion, diced
- 2 tablespoons olive oil
- 1 tablespoon Italian seasoning
- ½ teaspoon garlic powder
- ½ teaspoon dried thyme
- 5 carrots, peeled and diced
- 2 cups chicken broth
- 1 teaspoon ground black pepper
- 1 teaspoon salt

Directions:

1. Season meat with spices and set aside.
2. Add oil into the Instant Pot and set the pot on sauté mode.
3. Add onion into the pot and sauté for 5 minutes.
4. Add onion and broth and stir well.
5. Seal pot with lid and cook on manual high pressure for 40 minutes.
6. Release pressure using the quick release method than open the lid.
7. Stir well and serve.

Nutritional Value (Amount per Serving):

- Calories 788
- Fat 59.6 g
- Carbohydrates 5.8 g

- Sugar 2.8 g
- Protein 53.7 g
- Cholesterol 206 mg

Dijon Lamb Chops

Preparation Time: 10 minutes

Cooking Time: 10 minutes

Serve: 4

Ingredients:

- 1 pound lamb chops
- 2 garlic cloves, minced
- 1 tablespoon fresh basil, chopped
- ½ teaspoon garlic powder
- 2 tablespoons butter
- 1 teaspoon Dijon mustard
- 1 tablespoon olive oil

Directions:

1. Season pork chops with garlic powder and drizzle with oil.
2. Heat grill over medium-high heat.
3. Grill pork chops on hot grill for 4 to 5 minutes per side.
4. In a small bowl, mix butter, mustard, and basil.
5. Brush pork chops with butter mixture and serve.

Nutritional Value (Amount per Serving):

- Calories 295
- Fat 17.6 g
- Carbohydrates 0.6 g
- Sugar 0.1 g
- Protein 32.1 g
- Cholesterol 117 mg

Lemon Garlic Lamb Chops

Preparation Time: 10 minutes

Cooking Time: 10 minutes

Serve: 4

Ingredients:

- 1½ pounds lamb chops
- 5 garlic cloves, chopped
- 1 lemon juice
- ¼ cup olive oil
- 2 teaspoons oregano
- ¼ teaspoon ground black pepper
- ¼ teaspoon salt

Directions:

1. Add garlic, lemon, olive oil, black pepper, and salt in a large bowl and mix well.
2. Add lamb chops in a bowl and coat well with garlic mixture. Cover and place in refrigerator for overnight.
3. Cook marinated pork chops over a hot grill for 3 to 5 minutes per side.
4. Serve and enjoy.

Nutritional Value (Amount per Serving):

- Calories 434
- Fat 25.3 g
- Carbohydrates 1.8 g
- Sugar 0.3 g
- Protein 48.1 g
- Cholesterol 153 mg

Air-fried Meatballs

Preparation Time: 10 minutes

Cooking Time: 15 minutes

Serve: 2

Ingredients:

- 4.5 ounces pork, minced
- ½ teaspoon mustard
- ½ teaspoon garlic paste
- ½ tablespoon cheddar cheese, grated
- 1 tablespoon fresh basil, chopped
- ½ onion, diced
- Ground black pepper, to taste
- Salt, to taste

Directions:

1. Add all ingredients into the large bowl and mix well to combine.
2. Spray air fryer basket with cooking spray.
3. Make small balls from mixture and place in air fryer basket.
4. Air fry pork balls at 200C/400F for 15 minutes.
5. Serve and enjoy.

Nutritional Value (Amount per Serving):

- Calories 145
- Fat 7.2 g
- Carbohydrates 4.6 g
- Sugar 2.7 g
- Protein 14.5 g
- Cholesterol 2 mg

Chapter 12: Poultry

Crispy Chicken Tenders

Preparation Time: 10 minutes

Cooking Time: 25 minutes

Serve: 8

Ingredients:

- 3 pounds chicken tenders
- ¾ teaspoon cayenne pepper
- ½ teaspoon paprika
- 1 teaspoon garlic powder
- ½ teaspoon oregano
- 1½ teaspoon thyme
- 4 ounces pork rinds
- 2 eggs
- ½ teaspoon ground black pepper
- 1 teaspoon sea salt

Directions:

1. Preheat the oven to 200C/400F.
2. Line baking tray with parchment paper and set aside.
3. Add pork rinds to a resealable plastic bag and crush into breadcrumb size.
4. Add paprika, garlic powder, oregano, thyme, black pepper, and salt to the bag and shake well.
5. Pour pork rind mixture in a plate.
6. Beat eggs in a bowl.
7. Dip chicken in eggs and coat with pork rind and place onto prepared baking tray.
8. Bake in preheated oven for 25 minutes.
9. Serve and enjoy.

Nutritional Value (Amount per Serving):

- Calories 423
- Fat 18.8 g
- Carbohydrates 0.8 g
- Sugar 0.2 g
- Protein 59.8 g
- Cholesterol 213 mg

Shredded Chicken

Preparation Time: 10 minutes

Cooking Time: 20 minutes

Serve: 4

Ingredients:

- 1 pound chicken breast, skinless and boneless
- ¼ teaspoon oregano
- ½ teaspoon cumin
- 1 cup salsa
- ¼ teaspoon black pepper
- ½ teaspoon salt

Directions:

1. Season chicken with oregano, cumin, black pepper, and salt.
2. Place season chicken in Instant Pot.
3. Pour salsa over the chicken.
4. Seal pot with a lid and cook on manual high pressure for 20 minutes.
5. Release pressure using the quick release method, then open the lid carefully.
6. Shred the chicken using a fork.
7. Serve and enjoy.

Nutritional Value (Amount per Serving):

- Calories 234
- Fat 8.6 g
- Carbohydrates 4.3 g
- Sugar 2.0 g
- Protein 33.9 g
- Cholesterol 101 mg

Chicken Drumsticks

Preparation Time: 10 minutes

Cooking Time: 20 minutes

Serve: 6

Ingredients:

- 1½ pounds chicken drumsticks, skinless
- 1 teaspoon olive oil
- 1 teaspoon dried oregano
- 1 tablespoon apple cider vinegar
- 1 jalapeno pepper, halved
- 3 tablespoons cilantro, chopped
- 1½ cups tomatillo sauce
- ⅛ teaspoon ground black pepper
- ½ teaspoon salt

Directions:

1. Season chicken with oregano, black pepper, salt, and vinegar and set aside for 1 hour.
2. Place marinated chicken in Instant Pot and sauté until brown.
3. Add jalapeno, 2 tablespoons cilantro and tomatillo salsa.
4. Seal pot with lid and cook on manual high pressure for 20 minutes.
5. Release pressure using the quick release method, then open the lid carefully.
6. Garnish with remaining cilantro and serve.

Nutritional Value (Amount per Serving):

- Calories 161
- Fat 4.6 g
- Carbohydrates 2.3 g
- Protein 26.3 g
- Cholesterol 47.7 mg

Tomato Caper Chicken

Preparation Time: 10 minutes

Cooking Time: 22 minutes

Serve: 4

Ingredients:

- 4 chicken breasts, boneless
- 15 olives, pitted and halved
- 2½ tablespoons capers, rinsed and drained
- 2 cups cherry tomatoes
- 3 tablespoons olive oil
- Ground black pepper, to taste
- Salt, to taste

Directions:

1. Preheat the oven to 250C/475F.
2. In a bowl, toss together 2 tablespoons olive oil, capers, olives, and tomatoes. Set aside.
3. Season chicken with black pepper and salt.
4. Heat oven-safe pan over high heat.
5. Add remaining oil and heat until hot.
6. Place chicken in pan and cook until brown, about 4 minutes.
7. Flip chicken. Add olive and tomato mixture to pan.
8. Place pan in preheated oven and roast chicken for 18 minutes.

Nutritional Value (Amount per Serving):

- Calories 405
- Fat 23.4 g
- Carbohydrates 4.9 g
- Sugar 2.4 g
- Protein 43.3 g

Turkey Meatballs

Preparation Time: 10 minutes

Cooking Time: 20 minutes

Serve: 6

Ingredients:

- 1 egg
- 1 pound ground turkey
- ½ teaspoon cumin
- ¼ cup parsley, chopped
- ¼ cup onion, minced
- 2 garlic cloves, minced
- 1 tablespoon olive oil
- ¼ teaspoon cayenne pepper
- ¼ teaspoon cinnamon
- ½ teaspoon allspice
- ⅛ teaspoon black pepper
- 1 teaspoon salt

Directions:

1. Preheat the oven to 200C/400F.
2. Spray a baking tray with cooking spray and set aside.
3. Add all ingredients into the large mixing bowl and mix until well combined.
4. Make small meatballs from mixture and place on a prepared baking tray.
5. Bake meatballs in the preheated oven for 20 minutes.
6. Serve and enjoy.

Nutritional Value (Amount per Serving):

- Calories 187

- Fat 11.5 g
- Carbohydrates 2.1 g
- Sugar 0.1 g
- Protein 22 g
- Cholesterol 104 mg

Meatloaf

Preparation Time: 10 minutes

Cooking Time: 40 minutes

Serve: 6

Ingredients:

- 1 egg
- 1 pound ground turkey
- ½ cup sundried tomatoes, chopped
- ½ lemon zest
- ½ teaspoon dried dill
- ¾ cup spinach, chopped
- ½ cup onion, grated
- 1 teaspoon water
- 2 tablespoons tomato paste
- ¼ cup feta cheese, crumbled
- ½ teaspoon ground black pepper
- ½ teaspoon kosher salt

Directions:

1. Preheat the oven to 190C/375F.
2. Spray a loaf pan with cooking spray and set aside.
3. In a mixing bowl, add all ingredients and mix until well combined.
4. Transfer loaf mixture into the prepared loaf pan and bake in preheated oven for 40 minutes.
5. Slice and serve.

Nutritional Value (Amount per Serving):

- Calories 189
- Fat 10.6 g

- Carbohydrates 3.1 g
- Sugar 1.8 g
- Protein 23.3 g
- Cholesterol 114 mg

Garlic Chicken

Preparation Time: 10 minutes

Cooking Time: 40 minutes

Serve: 4

Ingredients:

- 2 pounds chicken drumsticks
- 1 fresh lemon juice
- 8 garlic cloves
- ¼ cup butter
- 2 tablespoons fresh parsley, chopped
- 2 tablespoons olive oil
- Ground black pepper, to taste
- Salt, to taste

Directions:

1. Preheat the oven to 230C/450F.
2. Grease baking tray with butter.
3. Place chicken on the prepared baking tray.
4. Season chicken with black pepper and salt. Sprinkle with parsley and garlic.
5. Drizzle lemon juice and olive oil over the chicken.
6. Bake chicken in preheated oven for 35 to 40 minutes.
7. Serve and enjoy.

Nutritional Value (Amount per Serving):

- Calories 560
- Fat 31.6 g
- Carbohydrates 2.9 g
- Sugar 0.4 g
- Protein 63.1 g
- Cholesterol 230 mg

Chicken Ranch Salad

Preparation Time: 10 minutes

Cooking Time: 10 minutes

Serve: 2

Ingredients:

- 1 cup cooked chicken, chopped
- ½ celery stalk, chopped
- 1 teaspoon rosemary, chopped
- 1 teaspoon yellow mustard
- 3 tablespoons ranch dressing
- 3 bacon slices, cooked and crumbled
- 1 teaspoon fresh parsley, chopped
- 1 teaspoon fresh basil, chopped

Directions:

1. Add all ingredients into the mixing bowl and toss well to combine.
2. Serve and enjoy.

Nutritional Value (Amount per Serving):

- Calories 143
- Fat 4.6 g
- Carbohydrates 2.8 g
- Sugar 0.9 g
- Protein 21.7 g
- Cholesterol 54 mg

Delicious Chicken Curry

Preparation Time: 10 minutes

Cooking Time: 20 minutes

Serve: 6

Ingredients:

- 1½ pounds chicken thighs, skinless, boneless, and cut into pieces
- 1 tablespoon jalapeno pepper, minced
- 2 tablespoons ginger, diced
- 2 tablespoons olive oil
- ¼ cup fresh cilantro, chopped
- 2 tablespoons fresh lemon juice
- 1½ teaspoons cayenne
- 1 teaspoon garam masala
- 1½ teaspoons turmeric
- 1 cup tomatoes, chopped

Directions:

1. Heat olive oil in a pan over medium heat.
2. Add jalapenos and ginger to the pan and sauté for 3 minutes.
3. Add chicken and sear chicken from both sides.
4. Add tomatoes and stir well.
5. Add all spices and stir well.
6. Cook until chicken is completely cooked, and tomatoes are softened.
7. Add lemon juice and stir well.
8. Garnish with cilantro and serve.

Nutritional Value (Amount per Serving):

- Calories 273
- Fat 13.5 g

- Carbohydrates 3.4 g
- Sugar 1.1 g
- Protein 33.4 g
- Cholesterol 101 mg

Chapter 13: Seafood

Basil Tomato Shrimp

Preparation Time: 10 minutes

Cooking Time: 10 minutes

Serve: 4

Ingredients:

- 1 pound shrimp, peeled and deveined
- 3 tablespoons olive oil
- 2 tablespoons fresh basil, minced
- ½ cup Gruyere cheese, grated
- 1 cup heavy cream
- 3 ounces sundried tomatoes, minced
- ½ teaspoon red pepper flakes
- 2 garlic cloves, minced
- Ground black pepper, to taste
- Salt, to taste

Directions:

1. Heat olive oil in a pan over medium-high heat.
2. Add garlic and red pepper flakes to the pan and sauté for 30 seconds.
3. Add sundried tomatoes and cook for 2 minutes.
4. Add shrimp and cook for 2 minutes on each side.
5. Add cheese and heavy cream and stir until cheese is melted.
6. Season with black pepper and salt.
7. Garnish with basil and serve.

Nutritional Value (Amount per Serving):

- Calories 301

- Fat 17.5 g
- Carbohydrates 4.1 g
- Sugar 0.7 g
- Protein 30.8 g
- Cholesterol 295 mg

Cilantro Lime Salmon

Preparation Time: 10 minutes

Cooking Time: 20 minutes

Serve: 2

Ingredients:

- 2 salmon fillets
- ¼ cup fresh cilantro, chopped
- 3 garlic cloves, minced
- 2 tablespoons lime juice
- 1 teaspoon lime zest
- ½ cup coconut oil, melted
- Ground black pepper, to taste
- Salt, to taste

Directions:

1. Preheat the oven to 190C/375F.
2. Season salmon fillets with black pepper and salt.
3. In a bowl, mix coconut oil, garlic, cilantro, lime juice, and lime zest.
4. Place salmon fillets in a baking dish. Pour coconut oil mixture on top of salmon fillets.
5. Place in preheated oven and cook for 15 to 20 minutes.
6. Serve and enjoy.

Nutritional Value (Amount per Serving):

- Calories 713
- Fat 65.5 g
- Carbohydrates 1.6 g
- Sugar0.1 g
- Protein 34.9 g
- Cholesterol 78 mg

Mediterranean Fish Fillets

Preparation Time: 10 minutes

Cooking Time: 5 minutes

Serve: 4

Ingredients:

- 4 cod fillets
- 2 tablespoons olive oil
- 1 teaspoon dried basil
- ⅛ teaspoon dried thyme, crushed
- ¼ cup olives, sliced
- 4 cherry tomatoes, diced
- Ground black pepper, to taste
- Salt, to taste

Directions:

1. Season fish fillets with black pepper and salt.
2. Heat 1 tablespoon olive oil in a pan over medium-high heat.
3. Add fish fillet in a pan and cook for 30 seconds. Flip fish fillets once.
4. Sprinkle fish fillets with thyme, olives, and tomatoes.
5. Turn heat to low and cover and cook for 2 minutes.
6. Add remaining oil and basil.
7. Cover again and cook for 2 minutes.
8. Serve and enjoy.

Nutritional Value (Amount per Serving):

- Calories 188
- Fat 9.2 g
- Carbohydrates 6.9 g
- Sugar 4.9 g
- Protein 21.6 g

Lemon Parmesan Shrimp

Preparation Time: 10 minutes

Cooking Time: 8 minutes

Serve: 4

Ingredients:

- 1½ pounds shrimp, peeled and deveined
- 1 fresh lemon juice
- 2 garlic cloves, minced
- 2 tablespoons olive oil
- ¼ cup Parmesan cheese, grated
- 1 teaspoon Italian seasoning
- Ground black pepper, to taste
- Salt, to taste

Directions:

1. Preheat the oven to 200C/400F.
2. In a bowl, add shrimp, olive oil, Parmesan cheese, Italian seasoning, and garlic. Toss well.
3. Transfer shrimp mixture on a baking tray and cook in preheated oven for 5 to 8 minutes.
4. Drizzle with lemon juice and serve.

Nutritional Value (Amount per Serving):

- Calories 214
- Fat 8 g
- Carbohydrates 2 g
- Sugar 0 g
- Protein 33 g
- Cholesterol 263 mg

Creole Seasoned Shrimp

Preparation Time: 10 minutes

Cooking Time: 8 minutes

Serve: 4

Ingredients:

- 1 pound shrimp, peeled and deveined
- 1½ teaspoons soy sauce
- 2 teaspoons dried parsley
- 2 tablespoons lemon juice
- 1 teaspoon olive oil
- 2 teaspoons Creole seasoning

Directions:

1. Preheat the oven to 230C/450F.
2. Spray a baking tray with cooking spray and set aside.
3. Add all ingredients into the mixing bowl and toss well.
4. Transfer shrimp mixture on a prepared baking tray and bake in preheated oven for 8 minutes.
5. Serve and enjoy.

Nutritional Value (Amount per Serving):

- Calories 164
- Fat 3.2 g
- Carbohydrates 6.4 g
- Sugar 4.7 g
- Protein 26.1 g
- Cholesterol 239 mg

Lemon Garlic Shrimp

Preparation Time: 10 minutes

Cooking Time: 8 minutes

Serve: 4

Ingredients:

- 1½ pounds shrimp, peeled and deveined
- 1 tablespoon fresh parsley, chopped
- 3 garlic cloves, minced
- 1 fresh lemon juice
- ¼ teaspoon red pepper flakes, crushed
- 1 tablespoon olive oil

Directions:

1. Preheat the oven to 200C/400F.
2. Spray a baking tray with cooking spray and set aside.
3. In a bowl, combine shrimp, red pepper flakes, garlic, and oil.
4. Spread shrimp mixture on a prepared baking tray and roast in preheated oven for 6 to 8 minutes.
5. Drizzle with lemon juice.
6. Garnish with parsley and serve.

Nutritional Value (Amount per Serving):

- Calories 238
- Fat 6.5 g
- Carbohydrates 3.5 g
- Sugar 0.3 g
- Protein 39 g
- Cholesterol 358 mg

Delicious Baked Salmon

Preparation Time: 10 minutes

Cooking Time: 15 minutes

Serve: 4

Ingredients:

- 1½ pounds salmon fillets, skin on
- 3 tablespoons dill, chopped
- ½ lemon zest
- 1 tablespoon olive oil
- ¼ cup fresh parsley, chopped
- ¼ teaspoon ground black pepper
- ¼ teaspoon salt

Directions:

1. Preheat the oven to 200C/400F.
2. Season salmon with black pepper and salt and drizzle with olive oil.
3. Place salmon on a baking tray and top with lemon zest, parsley, and dill.
4. Bake in preheated oven for 12 to 15 minutes.
5. Serve and enjoy.

Nutritional Value (Amount per Serving):

- Calories 264
- Fat 14.2 g
- Carbohydrates 2 g
- Sugar 0 g
- Protein 33.7 g
- Cholesterol 75 mg

Basil Pesto Salmon

Preparation Time: 10 minutes

Cooking Time: 20 minutes

Serve: 2

Ingredients:

For the salmon:

- 2 salmon fillets
- ¼ cup Parmesan cheese, grated

For the pesto:

- 3 tablespoons olive oil
- 2 cups fresh basil leaves
- 3 garlic cloves, peeled and chopped
- ¼ cup Parmesan cheese, grated
- ¼ cup pine nuts
- ½ teaspoon black pepper
- ½ teaspoon salt

Directions:

1. Add all pesto ingredients to the blender and blend until smooth.
2. Preheat the oven to 200C/400F.
3. Place salmon fillet on a baking tray and spread 3 tablespoons of the pesto on each salmon fillet.
4. Sprinkle grated cheese on top of pesto.
5. Bake in preheated oven for 20 minutes.
6. Serve and enjoy.

Nutritional Value (Amount per Serving):

- Calories 726
- Fat 57 g
- Carbohydrates 4 g
- Sugar 0.7 g
- Protein 49.7 g
- Cholesterol 108 mg

Chapter 14: Soup & Sides

Broccoli Soup

Preparation Time: 10 minutes

Cooking Time: 2 hours, 30 minutes

Serve: 4

Ingredients:

- 4½ cups broccoli florets
- 1½ cups cheddar cheese
- ½ cup mozzarella cheese
- ¼ cup cream cheese
- ¼ cup butter
- ½ cup heavy cream
- 2 cups chicken stock
- Ground black pepper, to taste
- Salt, to taste

Directions:

1. Add all ingredients except cheddar cheese and mozzarella cheese into the slow cooker and stir until well combined.
2. Cover slow cooker with lid and cook on high for 1½ hours.
3. Stir soup mixture well. Top with cheddar cheese and mozzarella cheese and stir until well combined.
4. Season with black pepper and salt.
5. Cover again and cook for 1 hour more.
6. Stir well and serve.

Nutritional Value (Amount per Serving):

- Calories 425

- Fat 37.4 g
- Carbohydrates 8.7 g
- Sugar 2.4 g
- Protein 16.3 g
- Cholesterol 113 mg

Roasted Mushrooms

Preparation Time: 10 minutes

Cooking Time: 15 minutes

Serve: 6

Ingredients:

- 2 pounds cremini mushroom
- 1 teaspoon fresh thyme, chopped
- 2 garlic cloves, minced
- 2 tablespoons coconut oil
- 3 tablespoons balsamic vinegar
- ¼ teaspoon ground black pepper
- ½ teaspoon sea salt

Directions:

1. Preheat the oven to 200C/400F.
2. Add all ingredients into the large mixing bowl and toss well.
3. Transfer mushrooms on a baking tray and spread well.
4. Roast mushrooms in the preheated oven for 15 minutes.
5. Serve and enjoy.

Nutritional Value (Amount per Serving):

- Calories 84
- Fat 4.7 g
- Carbohydrates 6.8 g
- Sugar 2.6 g
- Protein 3.9 g
- Cholesterol 0 mg

Parmesan Brussels Sprouts

Preparation Time: 10 minutes

Cooking Time: 10 minutes

Serve: 3

Ingredients:

- 16 Brussels sprouts, cut in half
- 1 teaspoon Parmesan cheese, grated
- 1½ tablespoons olive oil
- 1½ tablespoons butter
- 2 garlic cloves, minced
- ¼ teaspoon ground black pepper
- ¼ teaspoon salt

Directions:

1. Heat oil and butter in a pan over medium-high heat.
2. Turn heat to medium. Add garlic and sauté for a minute.
3. Add sprouts and cover the pan with a lid and cook for 10 minutes.
4. Top with Parmesan cheese and season with black pepper and salt.
5. Serve and enjoy.

Nutritional Value (Amount per Serving):

- Calories 159
- Fat 13.2 g
- Carbohydrates 9.8 g
- Sugar 2.1 g
- Protein 3.7 g
- Cholesterol 16 mg

Creamy Cauliflower Soup

Preparation Time: 10 minutes

Cooking Time: 23 minutes

Serve: 4

Ingredients:

- 1 medium cauliflower head, chopped
- 1 medium onion, chopped
- 1 tablespoon olive oil
- 4 cups vegetable broth
- Ground black pepper, to taste
- Salt, to taste

Directions:

1. Heat oil in a saucepan over medium heat.
2. Add onion and sauté for 3 minutes.
3. Add remaining ingredients and stir well. Bring to boil and simmer for 20 minutes.
4. Puree the soup using an immersion blender until smooth.
5. Season soup with black pepper and salt.
6. Serve and enjoy.

Nutritional Value (Amount per Serving):

- Calories 50
- Fat 3.5 g
- Carbohydrates 5.4 g
- Sugar 2.7 g
- Protein 1.5 g
- Cholesterol 8 mg

Garlic Mushroom Soup

Preparation Time: 10 minutes

Cooking Time: 25 minutes

Serve: 5

Ingredients:

- 20 ounces mushrooms, sliced
- 2 cups vegetable broth
- 5 garlic cloves, minced
- ½ onion, diced
- 1 cup coconut milk
- 1 cup heavy cream
- 1 tablespoon olive oil
- Ground black pepper, to taste
- Salt, to taste

Directions:

1. Heat oil in a large pot over medium heat.
2. Add mushrooms and onions in the pot and sauté for 10 minutes.
3. Add garlic and sauté for a minute.
4. Add broth, coconut milk, cream, black pepper, and salt. Bring to boil.
5. Turn heat to low and simmer for 15 minutes.
6. Puree the soup using an immersion blender until smooth and creamy.

Nutritional Value (Amount per Serving):

- Calories 252
- Fat 23.9 g
- Carbohydrates 9.4 g
- Sugar 4.5 g
- Protein 5.4 g
- Cholesterol 33 mg

Rosemary Roasted Radishes

Preparation Time: 10 minutes

Cooking Time: 32 minutes

Serve: 2

Ingredients:

- 3 cups radish, clean and halved
- 2½ tablespoons fresh rosemary, chopped
- 8 black peppercorns, crushed
- 3 tablespoons olive oil
- 2 teaspoons sea salt

Directions:

1. Preheat the oven to 220C/425F.
2. Add radishes, salt, black peppercorns, rosemary, and 2 tablespoons of olive oil in a bowl and toss well.
3. Transfer radishes mixture on a baking tray and bake in preheated oven for 30 minutes.
4. Heat remaining oil in a pan over medium heat.
5. Add baked radishes in the pan and sauté for 2 minutes.
6. Serve and enjoy.

Nutritional Value (Amount per Serving):

- Calories 220
- Fat 21 g
- Carbohydrates 8 g
- Sugar 3 g
- Protein 1 g
- Cholesterol 0 mg

Tomato Carrot Soup

Preparation Time: 10 minutes

Cooking Time: 1 hour, 10 minutes

Serve: 6

Ingredients:

- 2 tomatoes, chopped
- 1 carrot, peeled and chopped
- 1 tablespoon fresh ginger, grated
- 3 garlic cloves, minced
- 5 cups vegetable stock
- 1 onion, chopped
- 3 tablespoons olive oil
- 1 cup fresh coriander, chopped
- 1 teaspoon ground black pepper
- 1 teaspoon cumin
- 2 teaspoons salt

Directions:

1. Heat olive oil in a saucepan over medium heat.
2. Add onion, ginger, garlic, and carrots in pan and sauté for 5 minutes over medium heat.
3. Add tomatoes and chopped coriander sauté for 5 minutes.
4. Add remaining ingredients and stir well. Bring to boil.
5. Cover pan with lid and simmer over medium-low heat for 60 minutes.
6. Puree the soup using an immersion blender until smooth.
7. Serve and enjoy.

Nutritional Value (Amount per Serving):

- Calories 138

- Fat 10 g
- Carbohydrates 6 g
- Sugar 3 g
- Protein 5 g
- Cholesterol 0 mg

Chapter 15: Desserts
Yummy Brownie Bombs

Preparation Time: 10 minutes

Cooking Time: 21 minutes

Serve: 12

Ingredients:

- 3 eggs
- ½ teaspoon baking powder
- ¼ cup unsweetened cocoa powder
- ¾ cup Swerve
- ½ cup almond flour
- 2 ounces dark chocolate
- ¾ cup butter, softened

Directions:

1. Preheat the oven to 180C/350F.
2. Line 8*8 baking dish with parchment paper and set aside.
3. Add dark chocolate and butter in a microwave-safe bowl and microwave for 30 seconds.
4. In another bowl, mix almond flour, baking powder, cocoa powder, and Swerve.
5. In a large mixing bowl, beat eggs. Slowly add chocolate and butter mixture and mix well.
6. Now add dry ingredients mixture and mix until well combined.
7. Pour batter into the prepared dish and bake in preheated oven for 15 to 20 minutes.
8. Cut into pieces and serve.

Nutritional Value (Amount per Serving):

- Calories 174
- Fat 16.6 g
- Carbohydrates 5.1 g
- Sugar 2.7 g
- Protein 3.2 g
- Cholesterol 73 mg

Chocolate Fudge

Preparation Time: 10 minutes

Cooking Time: 10 minutes

Serve: 16

Ingredients:

- 6 ounces unsweetened chocolate, chopped
- 1½ teaspoons vanilla extract
- 3 ounces heavy whipping cream
- 7 ounces Swerve
- 8 ounces butter

Directions:

1. Spray 8-inch by 8-inch pan with cooking spray and set aside.
2. Add all ingredients in a microwave-safe bowl and microwave until mixture is melted.
3. Stir until smooth and pour into the prepared pan and spread evenly.
4. Place pan in refrigerator until fudge set.
5. Cut into pieces and serve.

Nutritional Value (Amount per Serving):

- Calories 177
- Fat 19 g
- Carbohydrates 4.3 g
- Sugar 0.2 g
- Protein 1.6 g
- Cholesterol 38 mg

Perfect Cheesecake Mousse

Preparation Time: 10 minutes

Cooking Time: 10 minutes

Serve: 5

Ingredients:

- ¼ cup Swerve
- 2 tablespoons peanut butter powder
- ¼ cup unsweetened peanut butter
- ¾ cup heavy cream
- 3 ounces cream cheese

Directions:

1. Add all ingredients into the large mixing bowl and mix using a hand mixer until smooth and creamy.
2. Pipe the mousse into serving cups and place in refrigerator.
3. Serve chilled and enjoy.

Nutritional Value (Amount per Serving):

- Calories 215
- Fat 19.8 g
- Carbohydrates 4.7 g
- Sugar 0.9 g
- Protein 7.2 g
- Cholesterol 43 mg

Quick & Easy Mug Cake

Preparation Time: 10 minutes

Cooking Time: 1 minute

Serve: 1

Ingredients:

- 1 large egg
- 1¾ tablespoons unsweetened cocoa powder
- 1 tablespoon granulated stevia

Directions:

1. Add all ingredients into the microwave-safe mug and stir until batter is smooth and well combined.
2. Place in microwave and microwave for 45 seconds.
3. Serve and enjoy.

Nutritional Value (Amount per Serving):

- Calories 93
- Fat 6.3 g
- Carbohydrates 5.5 g
- Sugar 0.6 g
- Protein 8.1 g
- Cholesterol 186 mg

Rich & Creamy Raspberry Ice Cream

Preparation Time: 10 minutes

Cooking Time: 30 minutes

Serve: 8

Ingredients:

- 5 ounces raspberries
- 1 teaspoon vanilla extract
- ½ cup unsweetened almond milk
- 1½ cups heavy cream
- ¾ cup Swerve
- 8 ounces cream cheese

Directions:

1. Add Swerve and cream cheese in a mixing bowl and mix using a hand mixer.
2. Add vanilla extract, almond milk, and heavy cream and mix well.
3. Pour mixture into the ice cream maker and freeze according to the machine directions.
4. Mash raspberries in a small bowl and add to ice cream once the ice cream is almost end of freeze time.
5. Serve and enjoy.

Nutritional Value (Amount per Serving):

- Calories 190
- Fat 18.6 g
- Carbohydrates 3.9 g
- Sugar 0.9 g
- Protein 2.9 g
- Cholesterol 62 mg

Choco Cream Cheese Fudge

Preparation Time: 10 minutes

Cooking Time: 10 minutes

Serve: 24

Ingredients:

- 8 ounces cream cheese, softened
- ½ cup Swerve
- 2 ounces unsweetened chocolate
- ½ cup butter
- 1 ½ teaspoons vanilla extract

Directions:

1. Spray 8-inch by 8-inch pan with cooking spray and set aside.
2. Add chocolate and butter in a small pan and melt over low heat.
3. Once chocolate butter is melted, add Swerve and vanilla extract. Stir well.
4. In a bowl, add cream cheese. Pour chocolate mixture over cream cheese.
5. Blend chocolate and cream cheese mixture using a hand mixer for 2 minutes.
6. Pour mixture into the prepared pan and spread evenly. Place in refrigerator until set.
7. Once it set then cut into squares and serve.

Nutritional Value (Amount per Serving):

- Calories 79
- Fat 8.4 g
- Carbohydrates 1 g
- Sugar 0.1 g
- Protein 1.1 g
- Cholesterol 21 mg

Easy Coconut Bar

Preparation Time: 5 minutes

Cooking Time: 5 minutes

Serve: 8

Ingredients:

- 1 cup unsweetened shredded coconut
- 7 drops liquid stevia
- 2 tablespoons coconut oil
- ½ teaspoon vanilla extract
- Pinch of salt

Directions:

1. Add all ingredients into the blender blend until well combined.
2. Pour mixture into the fudge tray and spread well.
3. Place in refrigerator for 1 hour or until set.
4. Once fudge is set, cut into pieces and serve.

Nutritional Value (Amount per Serving):

- Calories 65
- Fat 6.7 g
- Carbohydrates 1.6 g
- Sugar 0.7 g
- Protein 0.3 g
- Cholesterol 0 mg

Chocolate Mug Brownie

Preparation Time: 5 minutes

Cooking Time: 5 minutes

Serve: 1

Ingredients:

- 1 tablespoon unsweetened cocoa powder
- 1 scoop chocolate protein powder
- ½ teaspoon baking powder
- ¼ cup unsweetened almond milk

Directions:

1. Add all ingredients into the microwave-safe mug and stir until batter is smooth.
2. Place mug in microwave and microwave for 30 seconds.
3. Serve and enjoy.

Nutritional Value (Amount per Serving):

- Calories 80
- Fat 2.4 g
- Carbohydrates 6.6 g
- Sugar 1.1 g
- Protein 11.3 g
- Cholesterol 20 mg

Conclusion

Losing weight can be difficult. If you have tried several diets yet still don't see any measurable results, then let the ketogenic diet help you achieve your weight-loss goals.

This book is ideal for keto diet beginners. You have access to everything you need in this book to achieve success on the keto diet. This includes not only information for preparing recipes properly but also understanding the principles behind the keto diet. In this book, you will find 64 delicious and healthy keto recipes that are easy to prepare. Eat your way to your weight-loss goals with the keto diet. Good luck!